How do we learn?

We all learn in different ways. The Kolb Learning Style Inventory (LSI) is designed to help you understand how you learn best in educational settings and everyday life.

Learning can be described as a cycle made up of four basic phases. The LSI takes you through those four phases to give you a better understanding of how you learn. Knowing more about your learning style can help you understand:

- how to maximize your learning from educational programs
- how you solve problems
- how you work in teams
- how to manage disagreement and conflict
- how you make career choices
- how to improve personal and professional relationships

What does the LSI Workbook cover?

Section 1: Your learning – where, what and how?   2
- Your current situation   2
- Completing the LSI   2
- Recording your scores on the Learning Cycle   3
- Understanding the Learning Cycle   5
- Identifying your preferred learning style   6
- Scoring your preferred learning style   7
- Your Learning Style Grid   8
- What each learning style means   9
- The basic strengths of each learning style   10
- Strengthening and developing each learning style   11
- General tips for developing your learning styles   12

Section 2: Applying what you know about your learning style   13
- Solving problems   13
- Working in teams   14
- Resolving conflict   15
- Communicating at work   15
- Communicating at home   16
- Being a parent   16
- Managing money   18
- Considering a career   19

Section 3: Exploring your learning style further   21
- Experiencing: Identifying how you learn   21
- Reflecting: Exploring the many contexts in which you learn   22
- Thinking: Understanding the Learning Cycle   23
- Doing: Putting your learning into action   24
- Other useful resources   25

Your current situation

The LSI will be more helpful to you if you think first about a real situation. Take a few moments to reflect on a recent time when you learned something new.

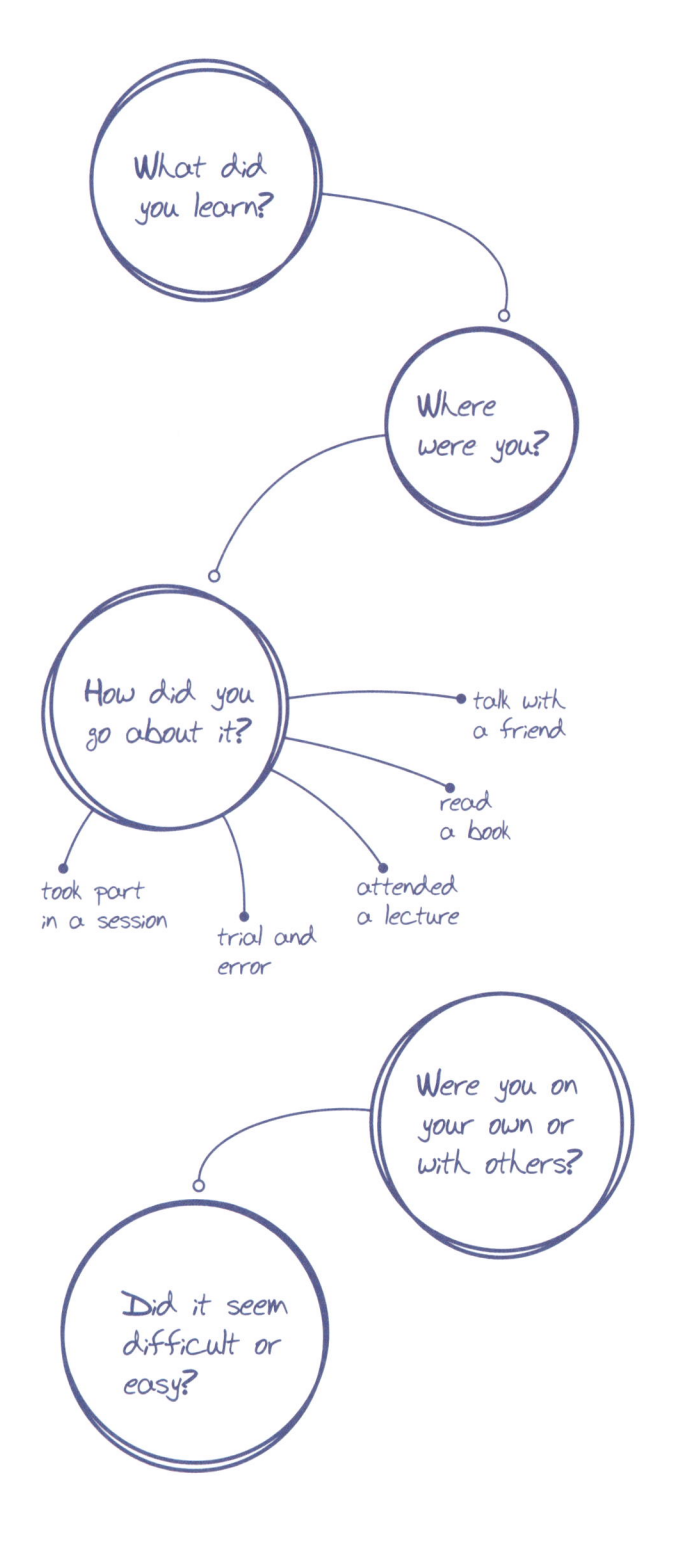

- What did you learn?
- Where were you?
- How did you go about it?
  - talk with a friend
  - read a book
  - attended a lecture
  - trial and error
  - took part in a session
- Were you on your own or with others?
- Did it seem difficult or easy?

Completing the LSI

- Now find the two-part questionnaire in this workbook. It asks you to complete 12 sentences that describe learning. Each sentence has four endings. To respond to these sentences, consider the recent learning situation you've just reflected on.

- Rank the endings for each sentence according to how well you think each ending describes the way you learned. Write 4 next to the sentence ending that describes how you learned best, and so on down to 1 for the sentence ending that seems least like the way you learned. Be sure to rank all the endings for each sentence. Do not give two endings the same number.

Some people find it easiest to decide first which phrase best describes them (4 – careful) and then to decide which phrase is least like them (1 – fast). Then they give a 3 to that word in the remaining pair that is more like them (3 – logical) and a 2 to the word that is left over (2 – happy).

> **Step 1:** Complete Sheet 1 of the questionnaire
> **Step 2:** Go to Sheet 2 to calculate your scores
> **Step 3:** Add up your scores for each shape
> **Step 4:** Enter your scores for each shape at the top right of Sheet 2

Each shape should have a score in the range of 12 to 48. Your four shape scores should add up to a total of 120.

Recording your scores on the Learning Cycle

On the diagram below, mark a dot on the corresponding line to indicate your CE, RO, AC, and AE scores. Then connect the dots to form a kite-shaped pattern on the diagram.

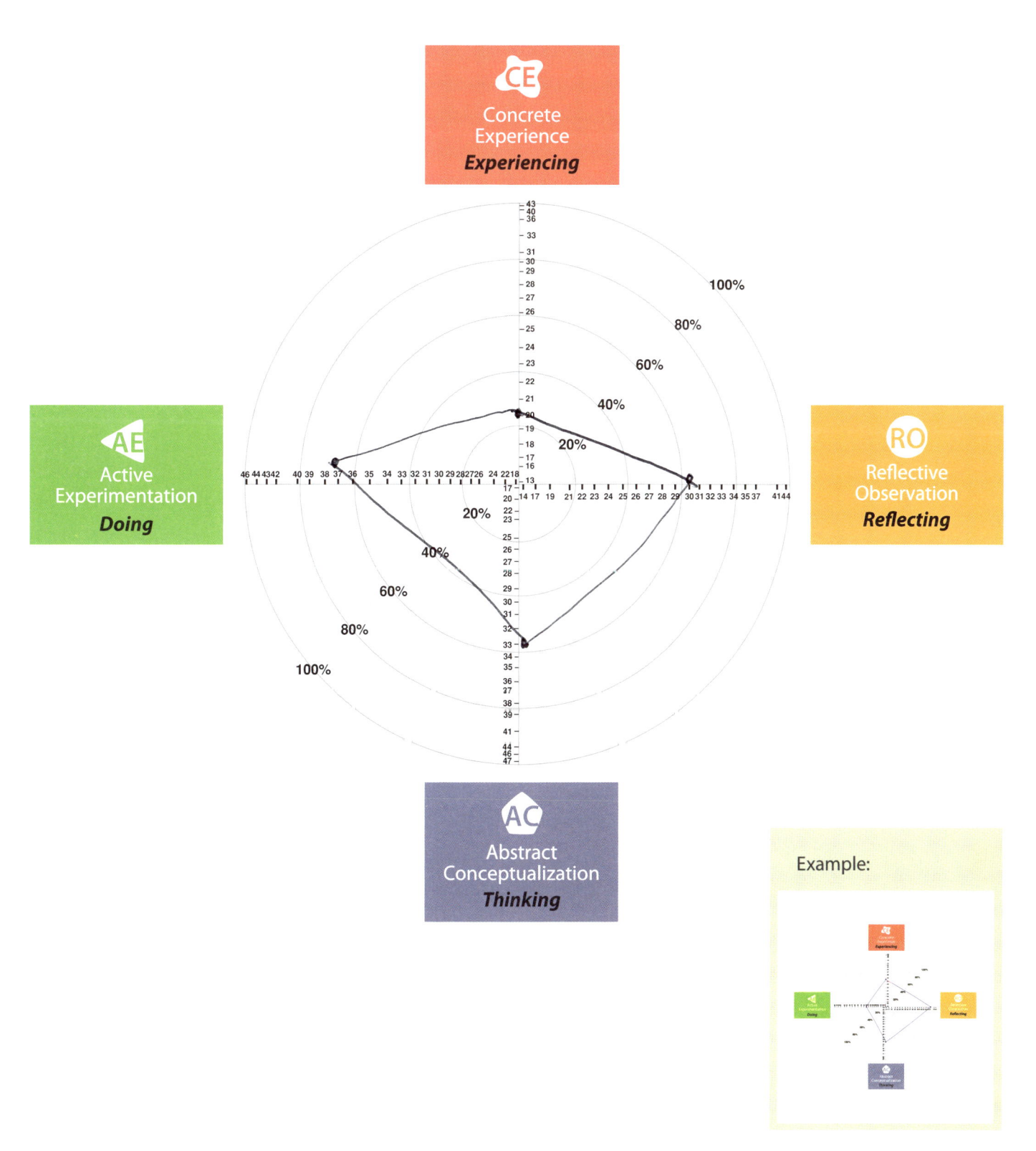

CE Concrete Experience *Experiencing*

RO Reflective Observation *Reflecting*

AC Abstract Conceptualization *Thinking*

AE Active Experimentation *Doing*

Example:

What do my scores mean?

Your scores indicate how much you rely on each of the four different learning modes: Concrete Experience, Reflective Observation, Abstract Conceptualization, and Active Experimentation. These learning modes make up a four-phase learning cycle. Different learners start at different places in this cycle. Effective learning eventually involves all four phases. You can see by the placement of your dots which of the four learning phases you tend to prefer in a learning situation. The closer your dots are to the 100% ring on the circle, the more you tend to use that way of learning.

What do the percentages mean?

Another way to understand the placement of your dots is to compare them with the scores of others. The percentile labels on the concentric circles represent the norms on the four basic scales (CE, RO, AC, AE) for 6,977 men and women ranging in age from 17–75.

For example, on the vertical line in the diagram (CE): if you were to score 26, then you would have scored higher on CE than 60% of the people in the normative sample. You can compare your scores for each of the other learning modes with the sample group.

Who is included in this sample group?

This sample group includes college students and working adults in a wide variety of fields. It is made up of users living in 64 countries, with the largest representations from US, Canada, UK, India, Germany, Brazil, Singapore, France, and Japan. A wide range of occupations and educational backgrounds is represented. For complete information about the normative comparison group and other validity research, consult the LSI Technical Specifications available at www.learningfromexperience.com or www.haygroup.com/TL

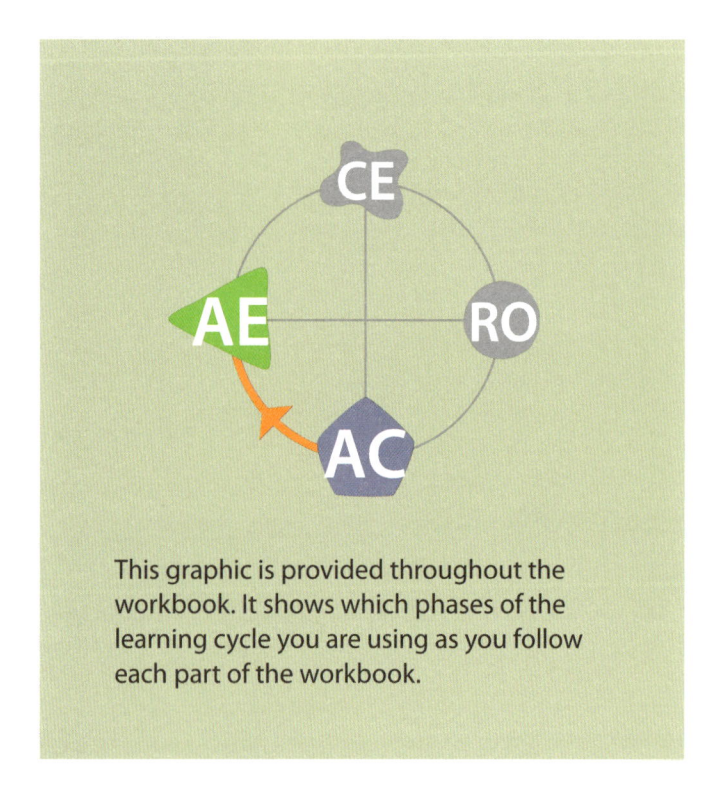

This graphic is provided throughout the workbook. It shows which phases of the learning cycle you are using as you follow each part of the workbook.

Understanding the Learning Cycle

The model below describes the four phases of the learning cycle.

There are two ways you can **take in experience** – by Concrete Experience or Abstract Conceptualization. There are also two ways you **deal with experience** – by Reflective Observation or Active Experimentation. When you use both the **concrete** and **abstract** modes to take in your experience, and when you both **reflect** and **act** on that experience, you expand your potential to learn.

Concrete Experience (CE)
Learning by experiencing
- Learning from specific experiences
- Relating to people
- Being sensitive to feelings and people

Reflective Observation (RO)
Learning by reflecting
- Observing carefully before making judgments
- Viewing issues from different perspectives
- Looking for the meaning of things

Abstract Conceptualization (AC)
Learning by thinking
- Analyzing ideas logically
- Planning systematically
- Acting on an intellectual understanding of a situation

Active Experimentation (AE)
Learning by doing
- Showing the ability to get things done
- Taking risks
- Influencing people and events through action

You may begin a learning process in any of the four phases of the learning cycle. Ideally, using a well-rounded learning process, you would cycle through all four phases. However, you may find that you sometimes skip a phase in the cycle or focus primarily on just one. Think about the phases you tend to skip and those you tend to concentrate on.

Identifying your preferred learning style

Now that you've plotted your scores on the graph (page 3), you can see that the connected dots form the general shape of a kite. Because each person's learning style is unique, everyone's kite shape will be a little different. The learning preferences indicated by the shape of your kite tell you about your own particular learning style and how much you rely on that style.

For example, if you have both Concrete Experience and Reflective Observation learning preferences, you will tend to have a Diverging style. Your preference may be to consider a situation from differing perspectives. You tend to diverge from conventional solutions, coming up with alternative possibilities.

> **If you have the Diverging style, your kite shape might look similar to one of these:**

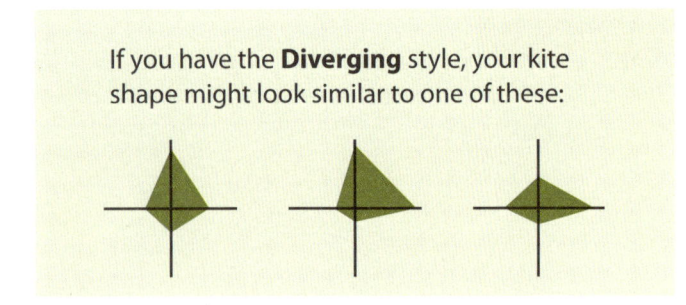

If you tend to use approaches that include Reflective Observation and Abstract Conceptualization, you probably prefer the Assimilating style. You may be interested in absorbing the learning experience into a larger framework of ideas. You tend to assimilate information into theories or models.

> **If you have the Assimilating style, your kite shape might look similar to one of these:**

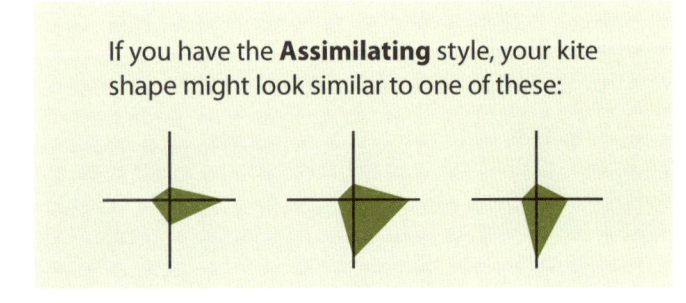

If you tend to approach the learning process by focusing on Abstract Conceptualization and Active Experimentation, you probably prefer the Converging style. You may enjoy gathering information to solve problems. You tend to converge on the correct solution.

> **If you have the Converging style, your kite shape might look similar to one of these:**

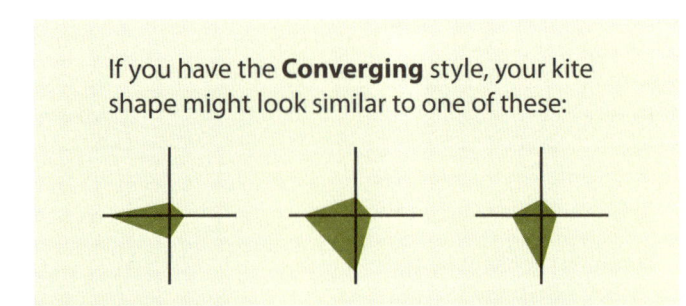

If your primary learning modes involve Active Experimentation and Concrete Experience, you may find yourself using the Accommodating style. If you prefer Accommodating, you may want to put ideas that you have practiced into action, finding still more uses for whatever has been learned. You tend to accommodate, or adapt to, changing circumstances and information.

> **If you have the Accommodating style, your kite shape might look similar to one of these:**

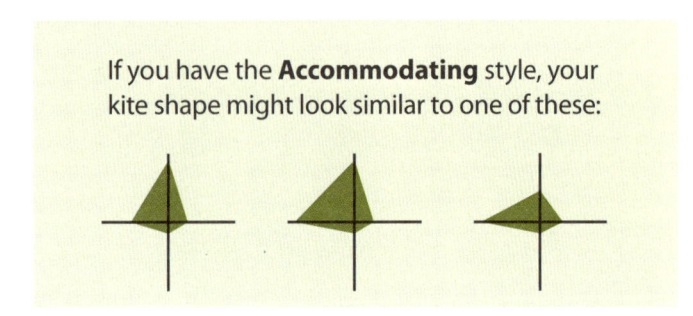

However, not everyone falls into one of the four dominant styles. You may have a profile that balances along two or more dimensions of the learning cycle. Current research suggests that some people learn through one or more of the 'balancing' styles. A balancing style may indicate a person who is comfortable with a variety of learning modes.

> **A few samples of a balancing style kite are shown below:**

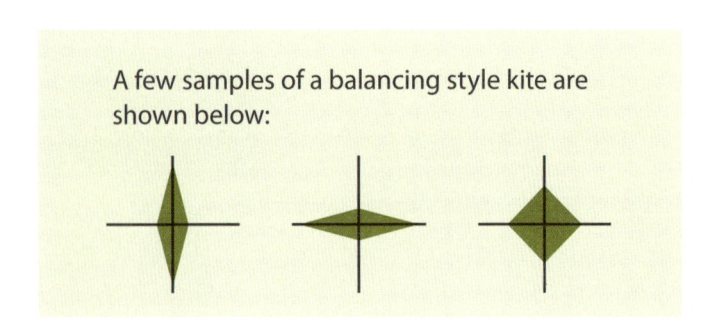

Scoring your preferred learning style

Understanding your preferred learning style, and the strengths and weaknesses inherent in that style, is a major step toward increasing your learning power and getting the most from your learning experiences.

To determine your learning style, take your scores for the four learning phases, AC, CE, AE, and RO (listed on the second sheet of the questionnaire) and subtract as follows to get your two combination scores:

Total for _33_ − Total for _20_ = _13_   This score tells you how you **take in** experience

Total for _37_ − Total for _30_ = _7_   This score tells you how you **deal with** experience

Now mark your AC-CE score on the vertical dimension of the Learning Style Type Grid on page 8. Mark your AE-RO score on the horizontal dimension. Then place a dot marking the intersection of the two scores on the grid

Example: If your AC - CE score is -2 and your AE - RO score is +15, your style falls into the Accommodating quadrant.

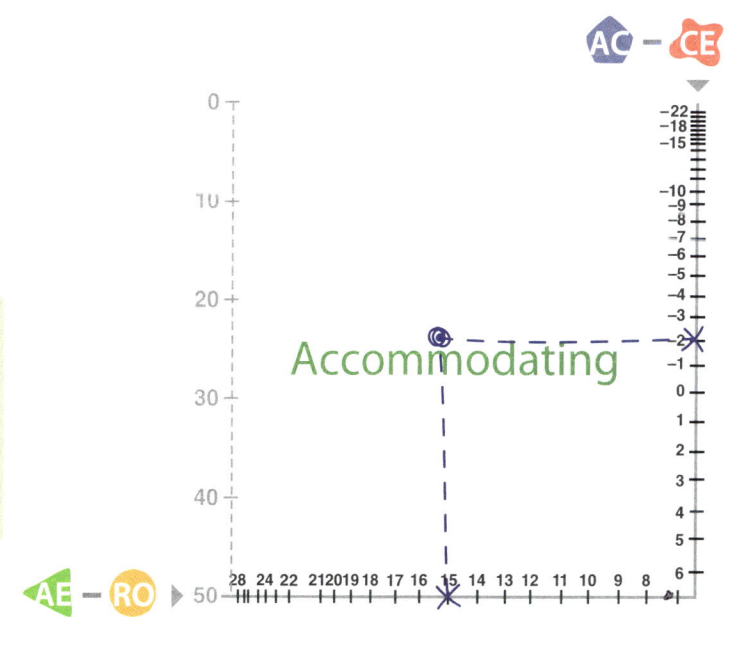

AC − CE

AE − RO

Accommodating

Section 1

Your Learning Style grid

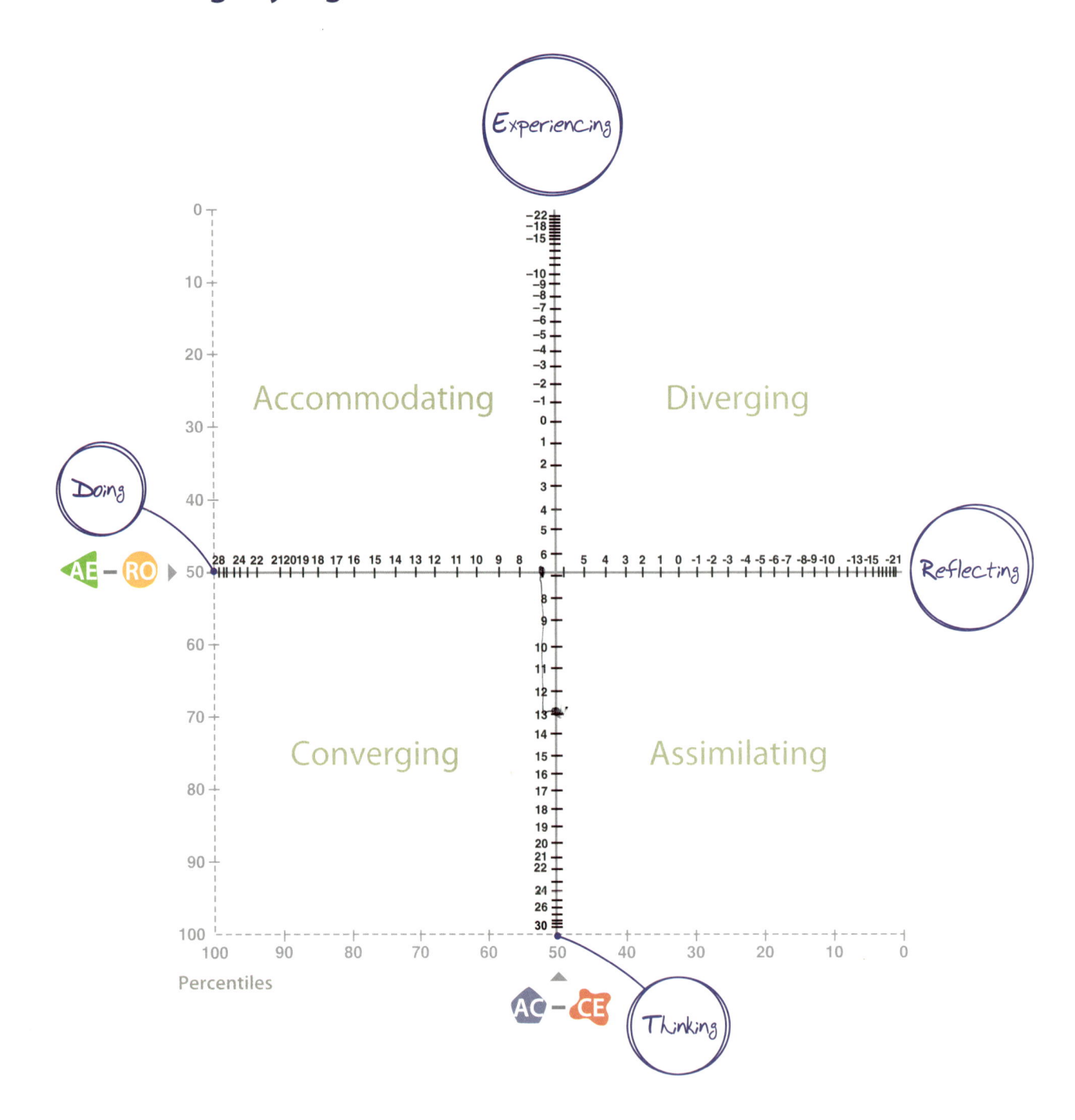

The closer your data point is to the center of the grid, the more balanced your learning style is. If your data point falls near a corner of the grid in the unshaded area, you tend to rely heavily on that particular learning style. If your data point falls in a shaded area then your style is characterized by a combination of the two adjoining learning styles. For example, if your data point falls in the shaded area between the Accommodating and Diverging quadrants your learning style is characterized by a strong orientation to Concrete Experience (CE) with an equal emphasis on Active Experimentation (AE) and Reflective Observation (RO), and with little emphasis on Abstract Conceptualization (AC). If your data point falls in the middle of the shaded area then you balance experiencing, thinking, reflection and action.

What each learning style means

The Diverging style

Combines the Concrete Experience and Reflective Observation phases

People with this learning style are best at viewing concrete situations from many different points of view. Their approach to situations is to observe rather than take action. If this is your style, you may enjoy situations that call for generating a wide range of ideas, such as brainstorming sessions. You probably have broad cultural interests and like to gather information. In formal learning situations you may prefer working in groups to gather information, listening with an open mind and receiving personalized feedback.

The Assimilating style

Combines the Reflective Observation and Abstract Conceptualization phases

People with this learning style are best at understanding a wide range of information and putting it into concise, logical form. If this is your learning style, you probably are less focused on people and more interested in abstract ideas and concepts. Generally, people with this learning style find it more important that a theory have logical soundness than practical value. In formal learning situations you may prefer lectures, readings, exploring analytical models and having time to think things through on your own.

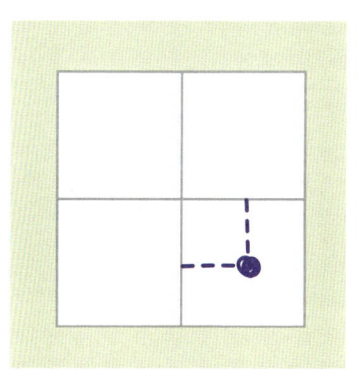

The Converging style

Combines the Abstract Conceptualization and Active Experimentation phases

People with this learning style are best at finding practical uses for ideas and theories. If this is your preferred learning style, you have the ability to solve problems and make decisions based on finding solutions to questions or problems. You would rather deal with technical tasks and problems than with social and interpersonal issues. In formal learning situations you may prefer experimenting with new ideas, simulations, laboratory assignments and practical applications.

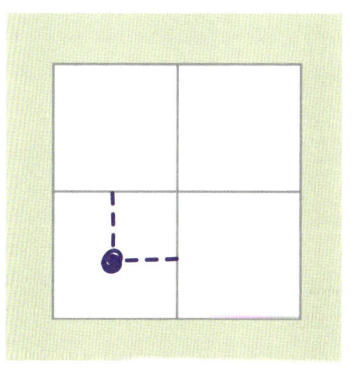

The Accommodating style

Combines the Active Experimentation and Concrete Experience phases

People with this learning style have the ability to learn primarily from 'hands-on' experience. If this is your style, you probably enjoy carrying out plans and involving yourself in new and challenging experiences. Your tendency may be to act on intuition rather than on logical analysis. In solving problems, you may rely more heavily on people for information than on your own technical analysis. In formal learning situations you may prefer to work with others to get assignments done, to set goals, to do field work and to test out different approaches to completing a project.

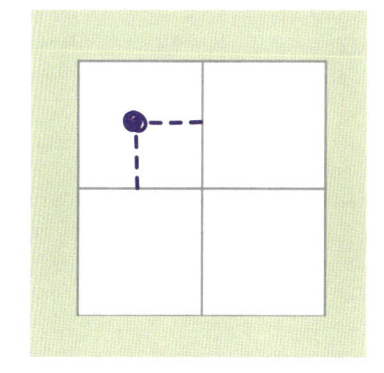

Note: The names of the learning style types are adopted from several established theories of thinking and creativity. Assimilating and Accommodating originate in Jean Piaget's definition of intelligence as the balance between the process of adapting concepts to fit the external world (Accommodating) and the process of fitting observations of the world into existing concepts (Assimilating). Converging and Diverging are the two essential creative processes identified in J. P. Guilford's structure-of-intellect model and other theories of creativity.

Section 1

The basic strengths of each learning style

The chart below identifies the strengths of each learning style.

Draw your own kite shape on this chart to help you see where your relative learning strengths are. You can also see those learning strengths that fall outside of your kite shape.

Are there areas not emphasized by your kite shape that you would like to develop?

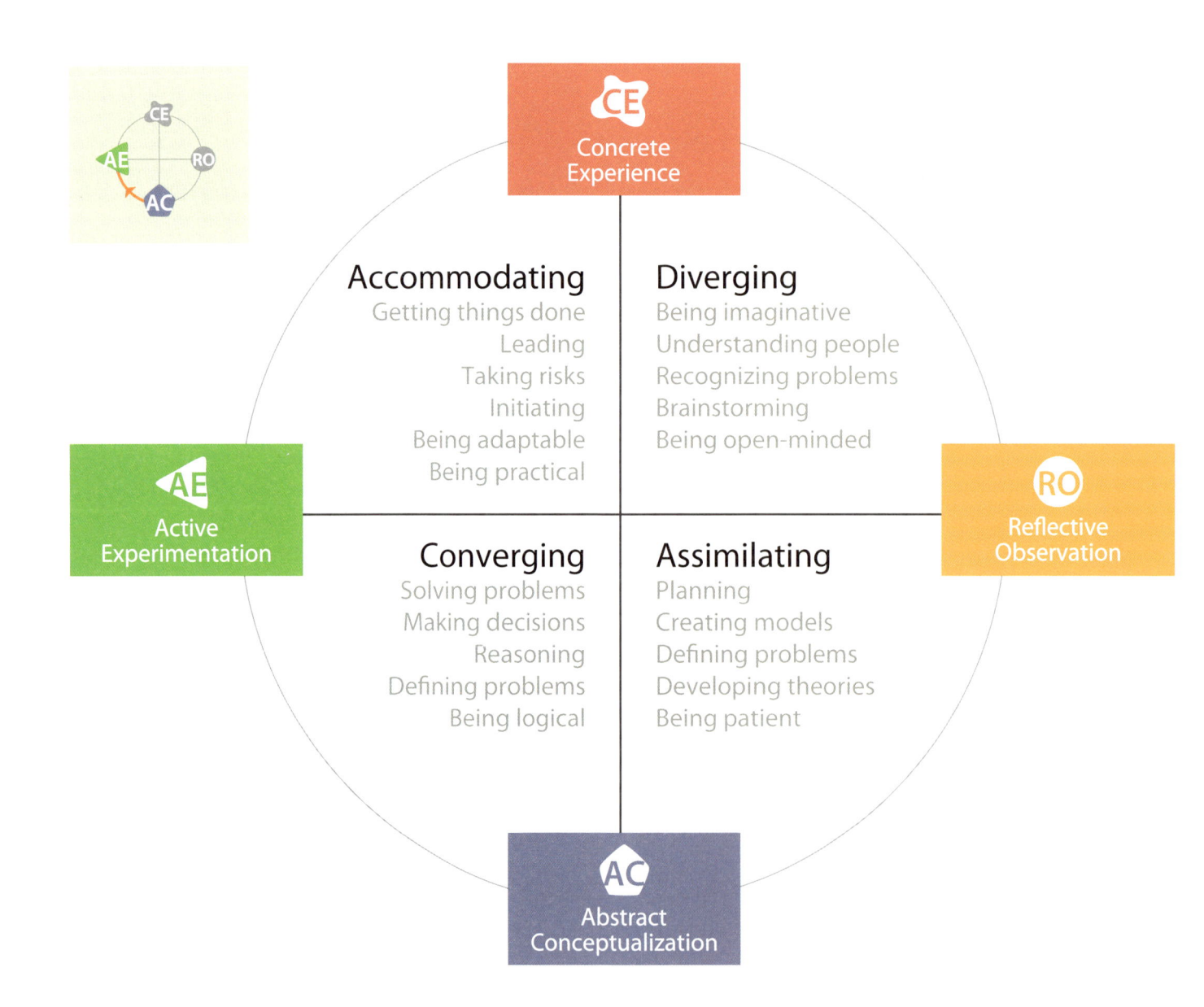

CE — Concrete Experience

AE — Active Experimentation

RO — Reflective Observation

AC — Abstract Conceptualization

Accommodating
Getting things done
Leading
Taking risks
Initiating
Being adaptable
Being practical

Diverging
Being imaginative
Understanding people
Recognizing problems
Brainstorming
Being open-minded

Converging
Solving problems
Making decisions
Reasoning
Defining problems
Being logical

Assimilating
Planning
Creating models
Defining problems
Developing theories
Being patient

Strengthening and developing each learning style

When you completed the questionnaire you thought about a real situation in which you learned something new. But remember, you are learning lots of different things in different situations; at home, at work, in your hobbies, in school, college or university, on training courses or with friends and colleagues. Different situations place different demands on us.

If you rely too heavily on one learning style, you run the risk of missing out on important ideas and experiences. So it's also helpful to consider how you use other learning styles.

For example, at work you may be a wonderful decision maker, but perhaps you see a need to strengthen your 'people skills'. At home you might be the one who always gets things done, but sometimes your actions need more planning, or perhaps you need more imagination in your day-to-day work.

Tips for strengthening your use of the Diverging style:

- tune in to people's feelings
- be sensitive to values
- listen with an open mind
- gather information
- imagine the implications of ambiguous situations

Tips for strengthening your use of the Assimilating style:

- organize information
- test theories and ideas with others
- build conceptual models
- design experiments
- analyze data

Tips for strengthening your use of the Converging style:

- create new ways of thinking and doing
- experiment with new ideas
- choose the best solution
- set goals
- make decisions

Tips for strengthening your use of the Accommodating style:

- commit yourself to objectives
- seek new opportunities
- influence and lead others
- become personally involved
- deal with people

General tips for developing your learning style

Whatever learning style you choose to develop, the following tips will help you:

Develop relationships with people whose learning styles are different from your own.

You may feel drawn to people who have a similar approach to learning. But you will experience the learning cycle more completely with those whose learning style is different from your own. It is essential to value different learning styles – problems are solved more effectively by working with others.

This is the easiest way to develop your learning styles.

Try to learn in ways that are the opposite of your current preferences.

Try to become a more flexible learner by consciously choosing to use the learning style opposite to your own preference. For example, if you have an Assimilating style, focus on using skills associated with the Accommodating style (taking risks, getting things done, being adaptable).

This approach may seem awkward to you at first – it is the most challenging approach to take, but it can also be the most rewarding. In the long run your increased flexibility will allow you to cope with challenges of all kinds.

Improve the fit between your learning style and the demands you face.

Concentrate on tasks that fit your learning strengths, and rely on other people where you have weaknesses. For example, if your preferred learning style is Diverging, spend your time gathering information and thinking of all the options. Get someone with the Converging style to choose the best solution.

This strategy can help you perform at your best and achieve greatest satisfaction.

Remember:
- develop a long term plan – look for improvements over months, not right away
- look for safe ways to practice new skills
- reward yourself – becoming a flexible learner is hard work!

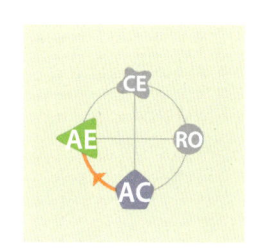

Solving problems

Understanding your learning style can make you an effective problem-solver. Nearly every problem that you encounter on the job or in your life involves the following processes:

- identifying the problem
- selecting the problem to solve
- seeing different solutions
- evaluating possible results
- implementing the solution

These processes mirror those in the learning cycle. Each process, or each piece of the problem, needs to be approached in different ways. Use the diagram below to identify your potential strengths as a problem-solver.

Circle your learning style and then notice the parts of the problem-solving process that correspond to it. Take some time to think about situations where your strengths as a problem-solver have emerged in the past. Then identify areas you want to develop further in the future. Notice the area that is opposite to your area of strength. Are there ways that you can develop your problem-solving skills in this area?

Working in teams

You have probably belonged to a number of teams. You know the ones that were effective and those that were ineffective. While a number of factors contribute to team effectiveness, learning styles, specifically a team's learning style profile, are a prominent factor. We are often most effective in our job when we work alongside team members with different learning styles who fulfil complimentary jobs.

For example, a person with a Diverging style working on creative projects in the arts field may be able to deliver most effectively because they work closely with a colleague with an Assimilating style who carries out careful project planning.

> Consider a team that creates an advertising campaign for a new product. Nearly all the team members prefer the Accommodating style. Consequently, they share a preference for action and rarely disagree. They quickly create and place an advert in an industry magazine. However, since the team lacks the more reflective Diverging and Assimilating styles, research and analysis that would have provided support for a targeted, direct mail campaign, for instance, are never considered.

Knowledge of learning styles can help you, as a team member, to assume a leadership role and guide the group through all the phases of the learning cycle. If you are a manager responsible for creating teams, this knowledge helps you ensure that all styles are represented and, therefore, all angles considered. In either role, you contribute to a more successful outcome.

Try teaming up with one or two of your colleagues or classmates. Choose an actual work- or study-related problem for the team to solve. During the process, note which team member is contributing ideas, who focuses on feelings and values, who tries to identify the problem, and who focuses on solutions. Are you missing any of the strengths associated with the learning cycle? If so, which ones?

Who might develop these strengths? How might they best be developed to serve the team? How can you adapt your group process to ensure that all phases of the learning cycle are included?

Better yet, try the *Kolb Team Learning Experience*. This resource helps teams to improve their effectiveness by making the most of the individual and collective potential of its members.

Resolving conflict

Conflict can be useful. The conflict that arises from differing perspectives helps us look at old issues in new, creative ways. Conflict can, however, become negative when disagreements are written off as 'personality conflict' or "I just can't get along with that person."

When you find yourself in a situation where there is a difference in perspectives, remember what you have learned about the four different learning styles. Use this information to elicit ideas, experiences and reflections from the other people involved.

> Consider the employee who publicly chastises a colleague for constantly holding up the department's progress by analyzing every detail of the job at hand. The colleague retaliates, saying that her accuser acts rashly, thereby jeopardizing the department's project. The two refuse to work together. Ultimately, the conflict extends beyond them to affect the entire department.
>
> An appreciation for different learning styles can alleviate this situation. Both employees may be right, but their learning preferences lie at the opposite extremes of the active-reflective continuum. They need to realize that the combination of their two styles is more effective than either style alone.

Communicating at work

Effective communication must overcome all kinds of potential tension. At work, this holds true for communication with your boss, colleagues, clients, and other stakeholders.

> Consider the Assimilating employee who is constantly frustrated by encounters with his Accommodating manager. As far as he can see, she pays little attention to the detailed facts and figures he carefully prepares for each of their meetings. She, on the other hand, is completely frustrated by the amount of detail and extraneous information he provides.
>
> In this situation, the employee would be better off presenting information to the manager in a bulleted, highlighted, "this is what I suggest" manner. In doing so, he would appeal to her learning preferences and get through to her in a way he never thought possible. On the flip side, the manager would benefit from an appreciation of different learning styles. She should acknowledge the work that the employee has put into preparing for the meeting and assure him that, although she is quite busy at the moment, she will make a point of looking through the information as soon as she has time.

Think of a situation where you could improve communication with another person at work. Perhaps the two of you have learning style differences. Do you prefer thinking things through while the other person prefers thinking on their feet? How can you combine your styles for a more effective outcome? How can you work together to develop each other's weaker styles?

Communicating at home

Work isn't the only place where communication can be a challenge. Different learning styles between family members can benefit, or hinder, the relationship. An awareness of your own and other family members' learning styles will help you appreciate the styles' strengths and understand their weaknesses.

Think about your own home situation. Is a family project (wallpapering, painting, cleaning out the garage, etc.) coming up? Can you find a way to combine your styles so that you can carry out the project more effectively? Can you help develop each other's weaker styles?

> Consider a couple assembling a bike. She has an Assimilating style and prefers to read the instructions, account for all the parts, and lay out the tools before she begins. He has an Accommodating style; he scatters all the parts around the room, immediately begins assembling the handlebars, and has no idea where the instructions are.
>
> To assemble the bike successfully, they need to combine their reflective and active styles. When both are represented, the couple can efficiently assemble a bike that is safe to ride.

Being a parent

Raising children is a serious business. In some cases it's a business entered into by two adults who have discussed their respective parenting philosophies seriously. In others, it is entered into without any previous discussion or meeting of the minds – or even self-awareness of the part our own learning preferences play in our parenting decisions. In either case, there will be moments when parents will bring some of their own learning preferences to bear on how they raise their children. Consider the following situation…

> Two parents have very different views on parenting. One favors allowing the children plenty of room to make (and learn from) their own mistakes, while the other prefers protecting them from mistakes.
>
> One prefers spontaneous activities – "Let's play it by ear, see what opportunities present themselves this weekend", while the other schedules structured activities – "We will spend Saturday morning at the Science Museum, followed by a trip to the park in the afternoon, and family dinner and board games in the early evening."
>
> One believes they will learn best from experiences (good and bad), while the other believes that you can address almost any issue (at no risk to the children) by informing (lecturing) them of the consequences associated with certain choices and actions, or providing them with reading material on the respective subject matter.
>
> One believes that it is their responsibility to introduce and expose the children to all that life has to offer, while the other wants to allow them space to see what personally interests them and what they naturally gravitate toward.

These parents may be approaching the situation based on their own preferred learning style – providing the children with the learning experience that they would prefer. Have they considered what the individual child would prefer? Do they realize the importance of helping the children strengthen their weaker styles?

In all likelihood, the children will benefit most from a combination of these approaches. They need the opportunity to experience, space to reflect, time to think, and the chance to experiment, all within a safe and supporting environment. As in most things, it is a matter of striking the appropriate balance.

Parents – together or with the help of friends and family – can make use of different learning preferences and provide a supportive environment in which their children learn. And they can consciously use the learning cycle to help the process along:

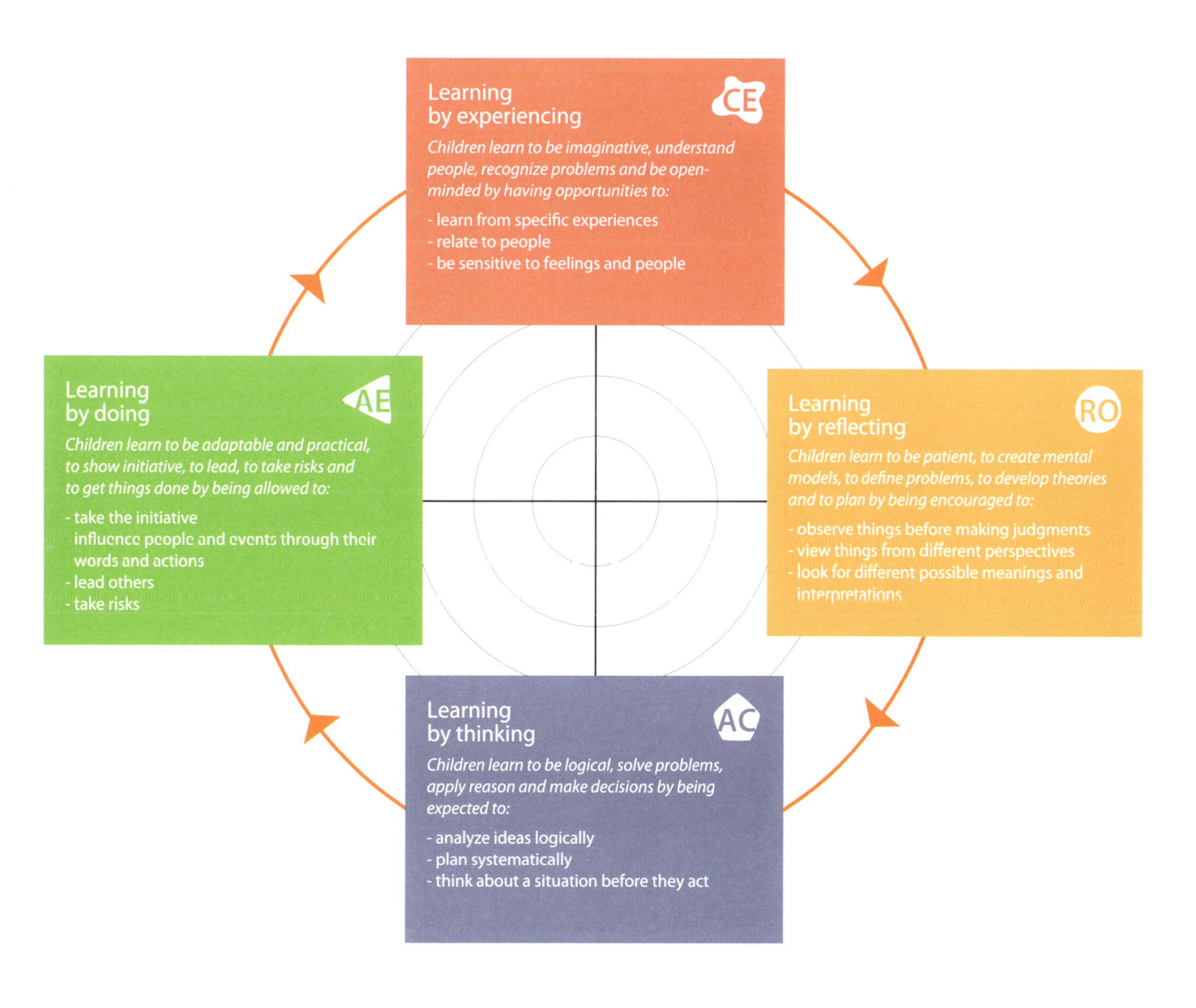

Learning by experiencing (CE)

Children learn to be imaginative, understand people, recognize problems and be open-minded by having opportunities to:

- learn from specific experiences
- relate to people
- be sensitive to feelings and people

Learning by reflecting (RO)

Children learn to be patient, to create mental models, to define problems, to develop theories and to plan by being encouraged to:

- observe things before making judgments
- view things from different perspectives
- look for different possible meanings and interpretations

Learning by thinking (AC)

Children learn to be logical, solve problems, apply reason and make decisions by being expected to:

- analyze ideas logically
- plan systematically
- think about a situation before they act

Learning by doing (AE)

Children learn to be adaptable and practical, to show initiative, to lead, to take risks and to get things done by being allowed to:

- take the initiative
  influence people and events through their words and actions
- lead others
- take risks

Managing money

People have very different views and opinions about money. For some people, money is simply for spending ('spendthrift'), while for others the decision to spend money of any sum is only made after painstaking consideration ('cheapskate'). When individuals with different philosophies about money move to a situation where they must share money decisions with each other, it can be quite challenging…

You've bought a house together. Big investment. Big commitment. But that was just the beginning. Now that you've been living together for some time, the debates have begun about home improvements. Your philosophy is, "If it isn't broken, don't fix it", while she thinks that it is important to invest in regular improvements to the property to keep it marketable and protect your investment. She is really pushing for establishing a home improvement fund that each of you contribute to on a monthly basis. You would rather make (and fund) repairs as the need arises.

The list is growing. She wants to paint the exterior – the color is so 70s. You don't necessarily like the color, but it's not chipping, it looks fine; you vote for leaving it as is. She wants to redo the kitchen. You, on the other hand, feel that while the appliances aren't top of the line, they are all in good working order. You vote for holding off until things start to break down. She wants to add another bathroom – people expect at least two bathrooms these days, but you feel that as there are only two of you and you work different shifts, one bathroom is plenty for you.

Striking a balance is in order. While the actual purchase of a home/property is just the beginning, it doesn't have to be the beginning of a never-ending outflow of cash just for the sake of it. You both agree that you want to protect your investment, but need to be flexible in choosing which investments will pay off, and in timing them in such a way that you can each manage them, along with other projects and expenses.

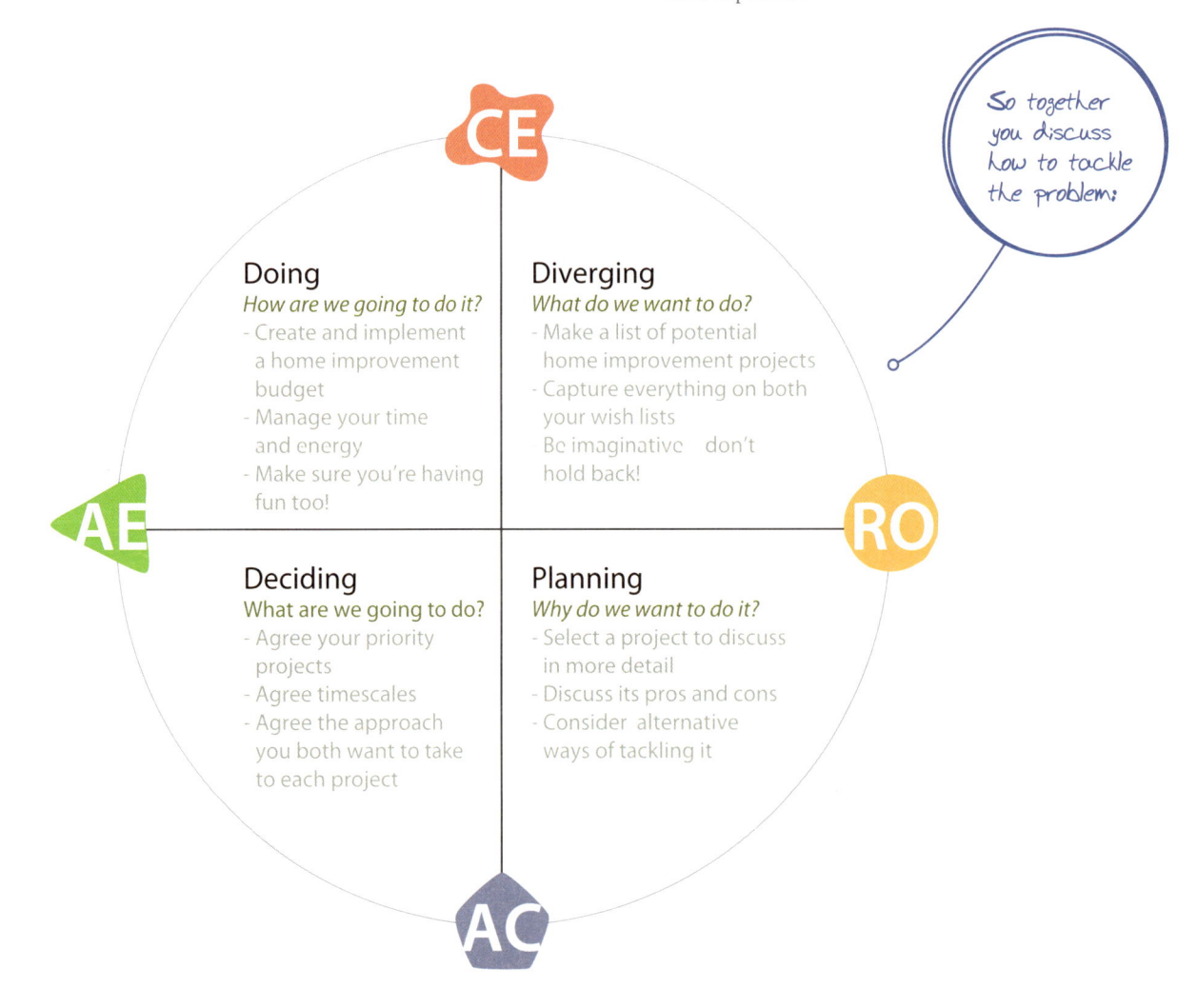

So together you discuss how to tackle the problem:

CE

Doing
How are we going to do it?
- Create and implement a home improvement budget
- Manage your time and energy
- Make sure you're having fun too!

Diverging
What do we want to do?
- Make a list of potential home improvement projects
- Capture everything on both your wish lists
- Be imaginative – don't hold back!

AE **RO**

Deciding
What are we going to do?
- Agree your priority projects
- Agree timescales
- Agree the approach you both want to take to each project

Planning
Why do we want to do it?
- Select a project to discuss in more detail
- Discuss its pros and cons
- Consider alternative ways of tackling it

AC

Considering a career

In general, people with certain learning styles tend to gravitate toward certain types of careers. However, within any career there are different jobs that lend themselves to a range of learning styles.

For example, a person with an Accommodating style who is practicing medicine may prefer the personal interactions and the active problem solving that a family practice entails. Someone with an Assimilating style may enjoy the medical science field, where research on medical problems yields the solutions that a practitioner may one day use.

We are often most effective in our job when we work alongside team members with different learning styles who fulfil complimentary jobs.

For example, a person with a Diverging style working on creative projects in the arts field may be able to deliver most effectively because they work closely with a colleague with an Assimilating style who carries out careful project planning.

People follow career paths that take different turns during their working lives. Our learning style reflects our preferences, but it need not constrain our future interests, preferences and strengths.

Note: The biggest mistake most people make when comparing their career with their learning style is to think that there is a formula that says, "My learning style is X so my career should be Y."

A better way to use the Learning Style Inventory when considering careers is to think about the characteristics of certain jobs that might suit your learning style.

You may also be interested in thinking about how your career can challenge you to stretch your learning strengths and help you develop new ones.

On the next page you will see the career characteristics that link to each learning style, along with a few examples of typical career areas. You can use this chart not only to explore new career opportunities but also to enrich your present career path.

The following questions may help you think about how your learning style relates to your career:

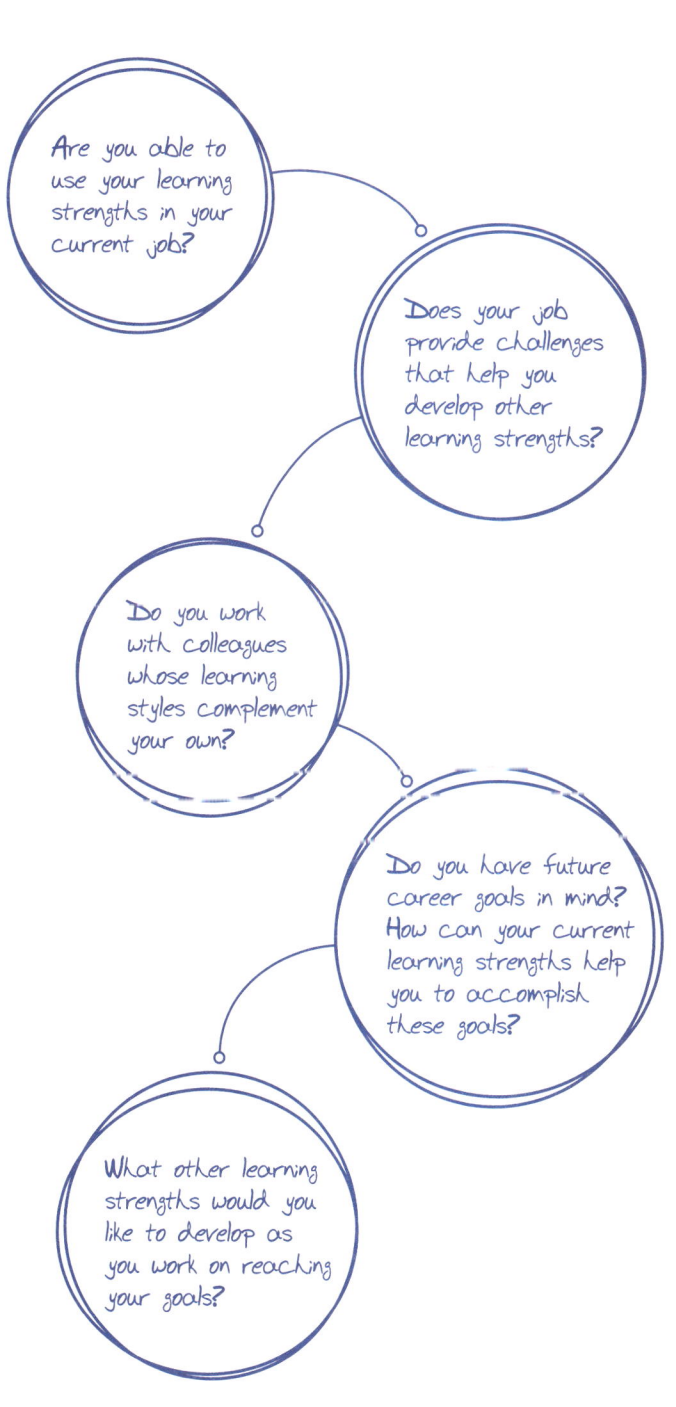

- Are you able to use your learning strengths in your current job?
- Does your job provide challenges that help you develop other learning strengths?
- Do you work with colleagues whose learning styles complement your own?
- Do you have future career goals in mind? How can your current learning strengths help you to accomplish these goals?
- What other learning strengths would you like to develop as you work on reaching your goals?

CE — Concrete Experience

Accommodating

Career characteristics:
- taking action – organizing day-to-day activities
- seeking out opportunities
- making things happen – taking risks
- implementing solutions to problems
- working directly with others
- influencing others – selling ideas, negotiating
- leading – inspiring and motivating others

These characteristics are typically – but not exclusively – found in action orientated careers, for example:
- management and human resources
- sales and marketing
- teaching, training, nursing, government

Diverging

Career characteristics:
- being sensitive to different perspectives
- communicating and building trust
- helping others
- dealing with ambiguity and variety
- gathering information from various sources
- being creative and making sense of things
- identifying problems and imagining implications

These characteristics are typically – but not exclusively – found in service careers, for example:
- arts and entertainment
- communications
- social service

AE — Active Experimentation

RO — Reflective Observation

Converging

Career characteristics:
- using systems and technologies to resolve problems
- experimenting with new ideas
- evaluating possible solutions
- making decisions – selecting the solution to a problem
- setting goals and checking progress

These characteristics are typically – but not exclusively – found in problem-solving careers, for example:
- computer science and engineering
- finance and economics
- applied sciences
- medicine

Assimilating

Career characteristics:
- gathering information
- investigating and researching
- organizing and interpreting information
- analyzing information – building the 'big picture'
- considering alternative solutions
- building conceptual models
- planning

These characteristics are typically – but not exclusively – found in information based careers, for example:
- sciences and mathematics
- social and physical sciences
- legal professions
- research and higher education

AC — Abstract Conceptualization

Section 3
Exploring your learning style further

This section of your LSI workbook is designed to help you explore your learning style more fully. It will help you to use the LSI to understand the ways that you, and others around you, learn. Like the main part of this workbook, this section is divided according to the different phases of the learning cycle.

Experiencing: Identifying how you learn

Go back to page 2. Focus on the real learning situation that you thought about there.

After taking the LSI, do you see that experience differently? How?

_____
_____
_____
_____

What new insights do you have into your learning experiences?

_____
_____
_____
_____

What kind of experiences did you focus on when you did the LSI? Were they physical experiences, like learning a new sport? Did you consider a work related task or some new learning in your personal life? Was it a more solitary activity that you learned on your own, or were others involved? Was this something that you learned for enjoyment, or were other things motivating you to learn?

_____
_____
_____
_____

Reflecting: Exploring the many contexts in which you learn

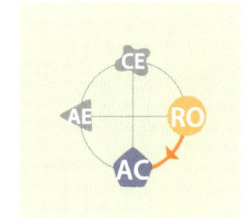

Learning never happens by itself. When you learn, you are always learning in some place, event, and time. Every situation you are in can be a context for learning. Typical learning contexts include places of work, family relationships, school, workshops and training programs, exploring a hobby, trying to figure out a new career direction and making and sustaining personal relationships. Your learning situations never stay quite the same. They change and grow as your personal relationships change, as job demands expand or as new opportunities come your way.

It is important, when reflecting on your learning style, to consider the many kinds of situations in which you are learning and all the kinds of things there are to learn. Your own learning approach may shift somewhat as you move from context to context. For example, communication techniques that you learn on the job may or may not be helpful when trying to resolve a disagreement with a family member. As you reflect on your own learning process, keep considering the rich variety of contexts in which you learn.

Consider the ways your learning approach changes in different contexts, such as home, job, school, friends, colleagues, etc. Make a note of your different approaches here.

Thinking: Understanding the learning cycle

You may want to remember that your 'place' in the learning cycle represents the dynamic ways that you are engaging in the learning process. The terms Concrete Experience, Reflective Observation, Abstract Conceptualization and Active Experimentation are not meant to be static titles that label you or your experience forever. Rather, they provide parameters for helping you to understand yourself more clearly in the learning process. As a learner, you never 'stay in one place'; your learning experience probably involves some experiencing, some reflecting, some thinking and some doing.

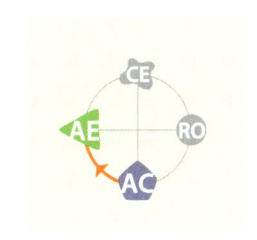

Because learning occurs in a cycle, the phases of learning occur time after time. You will probably find that you repeat the cycle several times as you encounter new experiences and revisit old ones. It's also important to remember that the LSI is not intended to be your only resource in understanding yourself as a learner; even this inventory doesn't measure your learning skills with 100% accuracy. You have many other rich learning resources around you. You can find out more about how you learn by gathering information from other sources, including your friends, family, teachers, boss, and colleagues.

Specify other sources that you might use to help understand yourself as a learner.

Doing: Putting your learning into action

Try out your new knowledge. Approach someone or something differently, based on what you now know about learning styles.

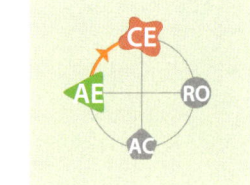

Write down your ultimate goal, the strategy that you will use, and how your success will be measured.

For example: If you're responsible for putting together a project team, your plan might start off something like this:

Goal	Strategy	Measurement of Success
To create a more effective team	Choose team members in such a way as to include learning style mix	Timely completion of team project within budget